A father and daughter's relationship
impacted by incarceration

DESTINEE THOMPSON

DADDY

i just wanted to tell you

CONTENTS

INTRODUCTION

If you ever happen to overhear a conversation between my daddy and me, your first impression may be, *wow they're close,* or *they seem to have a solid relationship,* and you would be correct. What you may not immediately pick up is that my father is incarcerated and has been physically out of my life since I was ten years old. Although our relationship is rooted in love, openness, honest reflections, and candid communication, the relationship took a lot of work! Building a relationship with a parent behind bars requires a level of honesty, transparency, forgiveness, and vulnerability that I wasn't quite able to grasp at ten years old. However, what I did know is there were so many things I wanted to share with my daddy, and there were very few ways to do it except tell him.

According to the National Institute of Corrections, in 2017, there were nearly 2.7 million children with an incarcerated parent in the United States, and more than

5 million children—7 percent of all **US** children—have had a **parent in prison** or **jail** at **some** point. Yet, in 1998 I felt like the only kid in the world who had a daddy that was taken away from her. No one ever talked to me about the feeling of isolation that came with having your daddy instantly snatched from your daily life, and no one gave me a roadmap for the journey ahead of me. Instead, I forged the unknown, alone, because I knew that a life without my daddy was a life I wasn't going to accept.

What you are about to read is an honest reflection of a Black girl's journey to build a healthy and meaningful relationship with a parent behind bars. The relationship I have with my father does not exist without deep hurt and disappointment; instead, I now recognize the pain that invited us to a level of transparency that may not ever exist otherwise. As years passed, we learned to evolve our relationship to shift and meet my need for a daddy to my need for a father. Even on March 15th, 2021, my father remains behind bars, and at 32-years, I still work to identify what a ten-year-old girl needs to tell her daddy. While also working to maintain healthy boundaries with my father. Although many years have passed, what remains the same is the special daddy-daughter bond we share.

This book isn't a how-to guide to cope with the impact of parental incarceration, because quite honestly, I don't think the emotional toll of parental incarceration is anything I have fully recovered from. Instead, what I am offering is a reflection of a daughter and her daddy's attempt to grow alongside one another despite the devastating impact of parental incarceration. What I know for sure is that we did not allow our circumstances to define how we would show up for one another, and despite every attempt to break our bond, I decided to tell my daddy.

I pray my reflection provides some little girl (or boy) consolation that they are not alone on their journey to building a relationship with an incarcerated parent. I hope you know that the pain, isolation, and grief you feel is real and deep, but not solitary. There are millions of kids around the United States experiencing the same thing, and I am one of them. I hope my journey illuminates the road ahead, and you find your light along the journey. I pray that you find your own way to say, daddy (mommy), I just wanted to say...

A LITTLE GIRL
AND HER DADDY

My 9th birthday was the best birthday of my life! I had a skating party at a local rink, and I invited my entire third-grade class. There was a clown, my third-grade crush, cake, presents, and of course my daddy! That day was so joyous. If I close my eyes, I can still recall the entire day, from start to finish. Yet, no one could have told me that memory would be one of the last with my daddy outside of prison walls. So, when my mom told me that my daddy would be going away for a long time, my mind immediately went back to my 9th birthday party—a time when life was simple and my daddy was there.

Me and my daddy waiting for the clown to begin her show

Even as a small child, my daddy and I always had a special connection. We would ride around for hours and just talk. I would be the only kid at the YMCA watching him and my uncles play basketball for hours. No matter the event, I just wanted to spend time with my daddy.

Me and my daddy on the dance floor at my great aunt's wedding

I could not contain the Joy
I felt the moment you was
born. You was truly a Godsend
You Keep my Spirit soaring
Destinee you are my Heart
Remember your Daddy Love
You More Than Anything

My
zines

Love
DADDY

Love

MY DADDY IN A VACUUM

Being the firstborn of my father's three children, I probably have more memories of the time I spent with my daddy before he was sent to prison. Yet, the memories of my father before his incarceration flicker faintly in my mind. What I can still vividly recall are the long drives to the middle of nowhere, waking up before dawn, the meticulous selection of outfits that adhered to the prison's ever-changing dress codes Waiting outside in the freezing cold or blazing heat hours before visitation hours. The intrusive and sometimes rude officers, the stale smell of a room packed with other families I did not know, and the long days of anxiously wanting to break free yet longing for every moment with my daddy. The memories of the prison visits and countless letter correspondences with my daddy are the memories that shape my childhood.

Even before I had words to articulate the mental impact parental incarceration has on children, I knew that my memories of jailhouse visits weren't anything I wanted to share with my friends. Instead, I went back to my 9th birthday, a time when life was happy and my daddy was there for everyone to see. What I wasn't able to fully articulate was the shame of spending my childhood weekends at a place that school and the world defined as bad. At ten, I knew my daddy wasn't a bad man, yet I was ashamed, so I put my daddy in a vacuum to the outside world.

Many of my childhood letters to my dad were centered around what I could recall about our life before he was sent to prison. I felt that if I could hold on to those positive memories and plan the next event for us to attend together, I could reconcile what the world said about the type of man my daddy had to be and who I understood him to be. Many of my letters (and photos) was my attempt to bring my daddy into my world. To include him in the joyous moments that were happening and longing for him to be a part of them with me. Also, it was my attempt to remove the shame of having a loved one in prison.

In the New Jim Crow, Michelle Alexander captured my unconscious attempt when she wrote, "Those stigmatized often adopt coping strategies African American once employed during the Jim Crow era, including lying about their own criminal history or the status of their family members in an attempt to "pass" as someone who will be welcomed by mainstream society" (Alexander, 116).

Even at ten, I adopted a coping mechanism, so many others before me had. Keeping my father in the vacuum granted me the acceptance of my peers. It provided me with an escape from my reality and provided me with a chance to feel "normal." Yet, years later, I recognized how that coping mechanism kept me in my own emotional prison. It would take well into my adulthood to free myself from the shame.

Dear Daddy,

My summer has been sort of borning. Only thing I have done is go to Six Flags 2 with my aunt but was sort of un fun. I've been taking pictures. they gave me at the end of the school year. I will send them to you when my mom has the money to get them devope. I really cant wait until I see you. I cant wait to see all the weight you have lost. I Love you daddy, and I always will. Daddy in your last letta you said Denia will be heresoon. Do you know when. Well see you soon!!!

Yours Truly
Destinee

Dear Daddy,

IT'S ME DESTINEE' . I'M OVER GRANDMA'S HOUSE .Iwas thinking about you so I SO IDECIDED TO WRITE YOU . SO I SAW YOUR PICTURE .YOU TOALLY DIFFERENT . I I LIKE YOU BETTER WITH HAIR ,BUT OTHER WISE YOU LOOK GREAT. DENIA TOLD ME THAT SHE CAME TO SEE YOU ON THE 7TH . I CAN'T WAIT TO SEE YOU . DADDY I DON'T MEAN TO SEEM LIKE I'M A REALLY BAD OF NEED OF CLOTHES ,SHOES ANDOTHER STUFF,BUT I DON'T WANT YOU TO WORRY ABOUT THAT YOU HAVE OTHER THING TO WORRY ABOUT . SO HOW IS THINGS GOING ? WELL SCHOOL IS GOING GREAT . I WANT TO TAKE TAPP ,& BALLET . SO HALLOWEEN

Grandma made us hold hands

IS COMING UP ,WHAT ARE YOU
GOING TO DO ? I'M GOING TO BE A
CHEERLEADER ,AND IMIGHT GO
TO AHALLOWEENPARTY ,ORGO
TRICK ORTREATING
WELLIGOT TO GO LOVE YOU
DESTINEE'

This was my first time ice skating; it was fun!

At summer camp, about to head off to the pool

*At Uncle Harold's house for the 4th of July, wish
you could've seen Lil Q almost drown*

Last day of school with my girl

I got so many toys!!

ROADTRIP BLUES

Looking back, I don't know what was worst, the silent shame or not talking about the horrible anxiety I felt going to the prison on weekends. Those trips to the middle of nowhere were like the best and worst of times. It was great because I got to spend face to face time with my father, but the process leading up to that time was dreaded, to say the least.

Throughout my childhood, my dad was always incarcerated out of state, in cities that I had never heard of. So at least once a month, my grandma would pile me, my brother, and my sister in the car and head down the road to go visit our dad. In the beginning, those trips were exciting because our grandma would buy us snacks, fast-food, and all the rap CDs my mom would never let me listen to. We would drive for hours to the middle of nowhere and stay in the only hotel (often motel) in town. Upon arrival, we would always pull out our planned visit outfits for inspection, and without fail, have to make a trip to the local Walmart to purchase something more suitable for the prison's dress code. The night before, we would have dinner, watch a movie, or spend time exploring the strange land the prison inhabited, but without fail, we would be in bed early in preparation for our earlier day ahead.

Like clockwork, before dawn, we would all wake and dress, still half asleep, and try to eat some semblance of "real food" before the journey to the prison. Every time I would have the anxious anticipation to see my daddy and share with him the latest things happening in my life at the time. Yet, without fail, that excitement was always a little damped by the arrival to the massively restrictive energy of the prison that housed my dad. In the few hours before we could actually see our daddy, my family and I endured the tenuous process of entering into the visitation room, momentarily experiencing your freedoms being stripped away. The process often left me feeling resentful and angry, but all that was wiped away when I saw my dad's smiling face come through the door.

For HOURS we would spend time talking, laughing, eating processed vending machine food, and playing board games inside the borders of the prison walls. The time felt like sand passing through an hourglass, and I couldn't help but watch the time pass by. Our visits ended with the obligatory prison photo in our partially fashioned Walmart attire. -Oh, how I hated those photos, as they were proof that my dad was not indeed in a vacuum, instead of a prison. Also, they never captured the painstaking attempt to look my best when I went to see my daddy; because at nearly every visit, my planned looked was co-opted by an impromptu adjustment to make it inside the prison. So, in every picture, I forced a smile to appease my daddy's request.

TEENAGE GROWING PAINS

While I spent most of my childhood trying to keep my father in a vacuum, my teens was when I prayed that my daddy would return to me. My teens were hard! Growing up, I always knew I had teenage parents, still growing and learning while trying to raise a child. Yet, I didn't fully grasp the impact of that until I myself became a teen.

Once I turned 15, my relationship with my mom started to take a turn for the worst. I spent many nights with tear-soaked pillows wishing that I could just go live with my daddy. Praying that he would come home, I could go with him, and everything would be alright. I longed to live with my father because my daddy understood me, my daddy listened to me, and my mom just didn't listen.

It would take a few years for me and my mom's relationship to rebound, but during that time, my daddy was there to support me in the only way he could, by listening to me.

A Father's Day
Message
From Your Daughter

"IF YOU
COULD LOOK
INTO
MY HEART..."

"A
father's
words of praise
and pride
are kept inside
the heart
to think of
time
and time
and time
again."

If you could look into my heart,
then maybe you would know
how many times I've thought of you
but haven't told you so.
And if you listened to my heart,
I'm pretty sure you'd find
that through the years
a lot of caring words have crossed my mind.
You can't imagine all the things
I feel and just can't say,
but you would know
if you could look into my heart today.

Happy Father's Day, Dad,
With Love

I love you Daddy and I always
will. Happy Father's Day. Destiné Thompson

Dear Daddy,

I didn't write you on my computer because my printer is broke. I'm on punishment for talking in class, but most of the time it wasn't me. I think I'm on punishment for 2 weeks. My teacher is mean, only teacher who's nice is Mrs. Stewart. Well enough of my complaining, how are you doing? I'm not doing so well, I feel like everything I do is wrong, like I'm stupid or something. I cry

"I cry my self to sleep.
miss you. I can't wait until
I want to hold you
let you go. Well daddy
gotta go my mom says I ha
to go to sleep. I LOVE YOU!

P.S. Please don't
tell anyone, Not
even my mom, or
I'll get in trouble

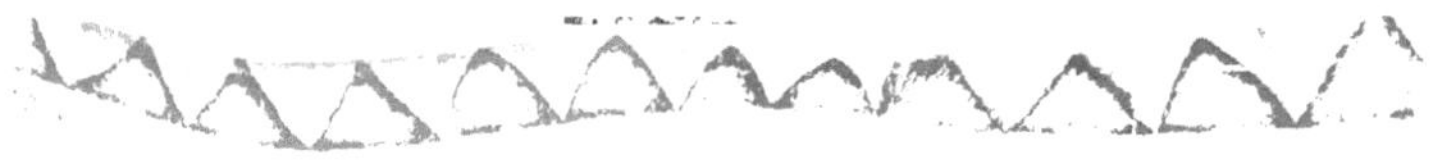

When it's easier to stay down,
some men choose
to GET UP.

When it's easier to be weak,
some men choose
to BE STRONG.

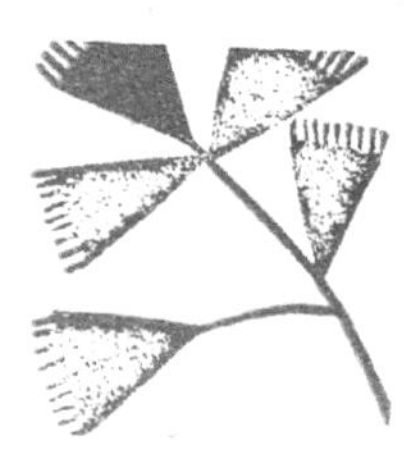

When it's easier to be afraid,
some men choose
to ACT COURAGEOUSLY.

When it's easier to remain deceived,
some men choose
to know the TRUTH.

When it's easier to flee,
some men choose
to STAY.

HONOR, INTEGRITY, and WISDOM
don't come from easy choices.
Take PRIDE today.
Your choices are CELEBRATED.

HAPPY FATHER'S DAY

Daddy,
The card said everything I could say and much more. I can't wait to see you. I'm proud to have a father like you. Have a great day!!

Destinee

By my senior year of high school, I would go to stay with my uncle (my dad best friend) and his family, and daddy played a huge role in that decision. Although staying with my uncle and his family provided a reprieve for the situation at home, I never quite felt at home.

During that time, I silently battled with depression, abandonment, and overall pain, while still working to graduate high school and be the first person in my family to attend college. During that time, I held on to the hope that the time was only a season, and eventually, joy would come into my life. I prayed that I would have the ability to love and trust again. I didn't feel comfortable or safe talking to anyone about my pain, so I turned to journaling. I journaled almost everyday to release the emotions and thoughts swarming through my mind.

monday April 16, 2007
I've been feelin really down lately
I just feel like a fish out of water.
Lately nothing's really goin my way
I lost my job mom treats me
like I'm doin her some injustice, m
dad feels the need all of a sudden
to teach me to be so self-sufficien
I live in a house with people who
aren't even my family (things that
I need/want I don't want 2 ask
them b/c they have their own
lives) family to provide 4, I went
over to my mom's 2day 2
get $ 4 my cap 3 gown pic's
and she starts 2 talk about
some hospital bill and what
insurence am I goin 2 have
once I go off 2 school. I just
feel like she's tryin 2 make
me feel bad 4 what she's
done 2 me. I feel like the
devil is bringing this spirit of
depression against me & I just
can't shake it. I know what
I need 2 do and I do have
2 do it, but I just can't
get it right. When I get
over one thing, here comes another

I know I gotta make it. I know I'm gon 2 make ~~it~~ it. The devil is just tryin 2 steal my joy. I don't wanna b that person who just throw my problems out of the window, and end it some other person, (stuck in my could've, would've, should've mood. I wanna make it so bad, 4 me that I can't even c straight, but these little things c comin now, and I can't have joy/peace. I'm grateful, Lord knows I'm grateful, b/c I know in the end it's only making me stronger but it hurts so bad. When the person who you want2 love u and show u the way can't love u, b/c they don't know how 2 love themselves and I want 2 give this love I have inside of me 2 someone, but I don't want 2 hurt. I have a lot 2 say, but I afraid no one will listen 2 what I say/the words won't come out right. I know I'm destined for greatness but I just can't get off this strom.

Once I entered college, I started attending church more regularly and read books that reframed my thinking like, The Secret, Who Switched off my Brain, and Woman Art Thou Loose, all of which led to an awakening. I started to explore what life must have been like for my mom, 15 and pregnant, how the experiences in her life shaped how she showed up as a woman and mother. I began the process of releasing pain and heartache. I began to understand the power of forgiveness and grace. Although I would love to say in those moments, my life instantly changed for the better, that is not the reality. I would go on to experience even more heartache and pain. However, what I can say is I established a solid foundation of reflection, empathy, and mindfulness that I still use today.

What I didn't know is that right when my mother and I began to mend our relationship, me and my daddy would have the biggest blow out of my life

MY DADDY IS JUST A MAN

During my teens, my daddy may have been my rock, yet during my college years, I harshly learned that my daddy was just a man with many flaws.

In the Fall of 2009, my daddy and I had a huge blowout. My dad's words were like a boulder to the chest, intended to take all of the wind from body. That year, again, I felt abandoned, betrayed, and disappointed, but this time the feelings were due to my daddy. During that time, every negative thing I had heard about him and his current inhabitation felt true to me. I was utterly devastated, and so I cut ties with my daddy, and he became another Black man behind bars to me.

Monday September 7, 2009
   Today I received an email from my father, and basically he called me a failure. He told me that everything that is happening to me is my own fault. He told me that I feel like people owe me something, and no one is going to give /owe me shit, basically b/c I have a horrible attitude. About a month ago I would have been devastated, but actually me feelings are the contrary. I'm actually having two emotions running through my body. The first is freedom/ expectations of God's total annoting falling upon my life. The second is hurt; of course I'm hurt b/c this is my dad talking her. The person you expect to stand behind you whether you are 100% wrong /right! I'm ok and I know where my ~~stren~~ strength and help comes from. I have a great power on my life and the devil thought he defeated me, but yet will I trust him. God will not let me hold my head down, b/c he has

me. He has prepared a table for me in the presence of my enemies. God shall get the glory in my life. He has to priviege Destinee and all the flesh attached to me, to get me where you only see him. Bishops sermon yesterday, was for me! God told him to tell me not to be sorry about those who left my life, yet be thankful for those who are still here. He told me to walk on to the abundance God has present/placed inside of me. He said he is steady placing & taking me through new tried to show how great he is in me. I know the promises in my life. I know what God has for me, and it's for his glory. He had to remove anyone who wasn't going to recognize him for the blessings. I'm excited

that God saw it fit to
choose a child of high school
drop out, a king pen's daughter,
a teenage single mother to
use me! I just pray that
he saves not only my father's
life, but his soul and mind
b4 it's too late. I just ask
that he save everyone that
is connected to his life. Allow
them to know, who their
God is. Forgive them father
for they know not what
they do. God have mercy
upon their soul. God keep
me under your blood and
keep me in your perfect
peace. I know and I
believe and trust you...
SO THAT SETTLES IT!

Amen!

Out of protection for my mental space, I didn't speak to my father for nearly two years. During that time, my father was briefly released from prison and I didn't see him or talk to him. It wouldn't be until after my 22nd birthday that I would learn that my father was re-incarcerated without us ever having the ability to connect in person. So I had a decision to make, accept that my daddy is a man, prone to mistakes, or allow the pain to control my life.

I decided to accept and recognize my father's humanity and began the arduous process of transforming our relationship from daddy and daughter to father and daughter. The process forced me to confront and openly share my pain and anger. While I was petrified of the vulnerability, I did not want to become a slave to pain, so I ventured into the unknown and told my daddy.

11/22/11

Hello,

Everything is good for me. I have about two weeks left of my last semester of classes! I am pretty excited about that, not as excited as I will be when graduation comes. Right now I am not 100% positive where I am going after graduation, but I have until may to decide. I know I am am leaving GA so that's one place scratched of the list. I know I have scratched PT school off my list, just because there's no room for growth except administration, and I definitely don't want to do that. I will continue on into some other form of rehabilitation, but again I am figuring everything will come to me when the time calls for it.

I am not really sure I could read the second part of the last page of your letter, but I will call your mom and see if she knows what you are referring to. About coming in December do you know the number I need to call, or should I ask her that too?

As far as the ball being in my court I understand that. Yet I also know if something is really important any reasonable person is going to persist even against opposition, but that's irrelevant. It doesn't make sense to dwell on the past. Instead be grateful for another opportunity to change the future. I would love for us to have a healthy relationship. One without regrets, no nothing will be perfect, but if we are honest enough to admit that, I know it can be one we both are happy with.

I never had a problem with talking about how I felt, but I didn't want to put myself in another vulnerable position. When I say vulnerable I mean for to not be disappointed again. I don't think you ever got a chance to know me. I know that's part of the circumstances and the other part others interpretations of me. I know you don't know me because of the things you would say to me. When everything went down. I felt as if you treated me like you treat everyone else instead of your child. I am not a person that sit around and wait for hand out, because I don't even like asking for help. So for you to even believe/say I act/remind you of Tamara is not correct. Nor am I a person bno makes a big deal about things going my way

, but people who don't know me can read my silence as me being upset. The people you listen to about me aren't even people I felt genuine enough to be my authentic self around. Out of everyone around you, I think the only person who slightly knew me was Kito, and to be honest was the person I felt I was hurt by more. I looked at him as a father figure, and the only one I really talked to. With you I have always thought that you treated people like pawns in your game. Everybody including you children had specific roles and if they didn't fulfill that role they could be removed. I don't believe it's something you do maliciously but you do it. I wasn't hurt by your actions or even your words. I think I was more hurt by the fact I had forced myself into believing I was different. Different in that you saw beyond your intentions and looked at me as your child. But I was wrong. When the whole situation went down you didn't come to me and even ask what happen; Instead you came and attacked (put me back in my place) Had you heard what I had to say maybe things would've been different. The situation w/ the people in the complex was a misunderstanding

The problem was, it was too many other people involed. My mom nor michelle had nothing to do with it. My reasoning for my mom calling michelle was to show how rediculis and unnecessary it is to have someone else, whose not involed in a situation speak / handle it for you. Just as you felt she had nothing to do with it. I felt the same with michelle. I had expressed ~~repeatedly~~ moultiple times now I felt about her, and only dealt with her out of respect for you. Was I wrong for handling it that way... sure, but then @ the maturity level I was @ it made perfect sense to me. From there the situation continued to spiral. I dont remember much, but I do vividly remember in an email from you. Stating quote", I won't be shit until I learned how to fix my attitude, and realized no one owes me shit / nothing" After that, that's when I decieided I didn't need any of that in my life. You said you blamed yourself for the way that I am. But I knew you didn't really know who I was, and if you did you would've have said the things you did. Now looking back, I am thankful for that experience, because after that I took a six month sabaticle, to find me

Not being in school I had time to read meditate pray, and learn (grow) into a woman. I don't blame anyone for my shortcomings. I just recognize them, and try to improve. I seperated myself from you and anyone associated with you because I knew it would be counterproductive to my growth. I had so much love and adoration for you, that I went against what I felt was best, and under no circumstances is that healthy. During that time I prayed for you and hoped that we could mend the broken relationship. I believe not until now, was either one of us ready. I have now laid it all on the line, and now placing the ball in your court. Hopefully we can learn and grow from our past.

Destinee

Our journey towards reconciliation required both of us to dig deep and address the hurt head on and learn new ways to share our fears and vulnerabilities. It wasn't until I became an adult that I began to think about how spending most of his formative adult years behind bars may have impacted my father. I no longer viewed my father through the eyes of a nine-year-old girl skating around the rink at my birthday party. For the first time, I saw him fully as a man who had his own personal experiences that shaped his life, who was actively processing the consequences of his actions and reconciling his own humanity behind bars.

Over the next few years, what I experience was a man, a father, actively working to restore his relationship with his daughter. He openly admitted his flaws without excuses and actively used his words to build up what he felt may have torn me down. I am so grateful for his words during that time.

As I continued to grow and evolve to Destinee Hattie Elaine Thompson, the woman. I had the opportunity to get to know Quentin Jerome Thompson Sr., the man, my father.

1-26-14

This is not just a thank you card, because I have so many feelings I love to share with you. I'm so proud of the young lady you have grown to be. The beautiful woman you is today. You always been a good loving girl, but now you is a hottie! :) I'm just the proudest father because of you. You is all I ever dream a perfect daughter would be. Thank you for allowing me to be in your life. I haven't been a good dad, and it's only because of you that we have any kind of relationship. It is going to take a life time to make up, but I will die trying.

2014

I feel you is a star everyday! You always been a star, and I knew it from the day you was born. To watch you grow into this great woman is a blessing. I'm so proud of you on all levels. I could not ask for a better daughter. Don't let nothing or no one dull your shine. You was born to be a leader, and now is your time to take control of your life and put it on the path to your endgame. Make this year the first chapter of your new book of life. Set goals big and small for this year, and do what it take to get them done. This is your time! Just Shine Baby!!!! I believe in you not because you is my daughter, because I know a Star when I see one!

1-5-16

Well Hello Des., hope this year already have a good feeling to it. I feel okay, but want to get a few months down before I can tell how it will go. I really feel you about taken the next step in life to get your career going. I know you feel like you don't have all you need to do what you need to get things moving. You might lack confidence that you can reach this outcome, but believe in yourself and have faith that God have this plan for you. If you believe, then it will not be so hard to do. I'm so proud of you for the woman you have become, but I know you have so much more to do with your life and bless this world with. I always seen you as a doctor since you 1st told me in the car. Make it happen, and be a leader for so many other young black women. Plus you will be able to help so many with this gift. It's so many people need a good/great caring doc, and you can be this for so many!

Love You

10-24-2018

I really hope you know how much I love and respect you. To watch you grow into the woman you is today is no shock. I always knew that you was mark for greatness! Everything you think, dream, or feel is here for you. You cant be stop! No one can stop your shine. Success is your birth right. As long as you put one foot in front of the other you will get to the top of any mountain. I'm not telling you anything you don't feel down in your soul. Your name say it all. Love You

Destinee Thompson

QUENTIN JEROME THOMPSON SR., THE MAN, MY FATHER

Once my father and I reconciled, our relationship evolved on so many levels; he became my friend, my confidant, and my father. I found myself talking to him about EVERYTHING, work, friendships, relationships, sex, travel, his childhood, and his dating history. I learned so much from him daily; it's unreal. My dad has become my sensei. I always felt a special connection, but now that connection transcends many areas of my life.

During our conversations, I learned about his childhood trauma and the impact of growing up poor and Black in America during the 70's and 80's. How at 13, he could never have imagined he would live to see 21, so everyday after his 21st birthday, he felt he was living on borrowed time. I learned how growing up without a father in his life; gangs and street culture provided the male influence he longed for. I learned that my father was a chauvinist and a romantic person, all wrapped in one. Even in his 40's and behind bars, he still possesses a level of charm that can make anyone feel like they are the center of the universe. He's told me about his fears and disappointments as a father. Listening to my daddy's honest reflections empowers me to own my own story and tell my truth.

Although I can't put into words everything that I have learned from my father, I can say is that even though he has spent most of his young adult life behind bars, his mind has never been incarcerated. I talk to my dad sometimes and I think to myself, dang, how does he know that and I don't. My father has a beautiful mind, and under different circumstances, he could have been the CEO of any major corporation. My father's impact on other people's lives still resounds today. Anyone who has ever come in contact with my father speaks about the impact his word, actions, or presence had on their lives.

I know I said I can't articulate everything my dad taught me, here is my attempt to capture some of the lessons I've picked up through the years:

1. A person will only do what you allow/require them to do.

2. Sometimes you have to put the fire under a person's ass to see what they are really about.

3. As a leader, you must be able to see and communicate at every level.

4. Kindness and communication can get you anything- you should treat the janitor and the CEO like the same person.

5. People never forget how you make them feel, no matter how long it's been.

6. Keep working on the plan; eventually, you will see the manifestation of your work.

7. Everyone wants to be needed.

8. Set your expectations but live your life- expectations are goals/daily habits, but you should not let them interfere with your ability to live life.

9. Work hard, Play harder, Treat yourself and others.

10. As a woman, get to your own bag! If a man is threatened by it, he isn't the man for me.

11. Forgiveness is critical.

12. It all starts with a mindset.

13. Sometimes you have to work the vision before others buy into the vision.

14. When a person has a perception of you in their mind, that's all they can view you from, and you have to work 10X harder to change a negative perception.

15. I am a star, and greatness is my birthright (I knew it, but to hear it affirmed is phenomenal).

12-2-2020

Daddy,
        I know the recent news was
what we desired, but I want you
to know, no matter what a judge/
DA/ the government says about you
and your character. I want you
to know I see and admire the
change. You said that when a
person sees you in a particular
light it becomes harder/ nearly
impossible to change that narrative.
Although changes other people's heart
and mind may be difficult, don't
let it deter you. Despite the
circumstances you have never
let your mind become imprisioned.
You are always pushing yourself to
evolve and grow. You are a natural
leader and based on a combination
of enviornment and need you began
your journey down a road that
led to difficult ends. However as you
have matured as a man, your
recognized that if you and others
had different opportunities things
would've been different. In this
current chapter I see you seeking
opportunities to shift the paradigm
for yourself and other. I know you

have the ingredients to be a powerful change agent (credibility + relatability+ vision + plan for the future) and a calling to bridge the gap. Use this temporary set back as an opportunity to hone that strategy. Stay focused, keep your energy high, and continuously evaluate. I also believe there is an invitation to evaluate internal and external forces that may stand in your way to achieving your purpose. Examine, evaluate, and adjust accordingly. Nothing catches you by surprise. Now we know, so now you know what you must do moving forward. Continue down your path. I have heard your passion to want to help and lead others. That work can start right now. I know being here would make the process easy, but it's not impossible. Luckily the current environment is keeping all of us inside, so write, leverage those of us who share your vision, and innovate. As a people we have always found a way, and this situation is no different. Finally daddy I want you to know that Quentin Jerome Thompson SR. is a man!

A man of vision. A man of purpose. A man of pride. A man of wisdom. A man w/ a heart for those he love. A man who has amazing foresight. A man w/ charisma. A man of impact. A man w/ passion. A man who love. A man who is loved. A man of value, and most important a father.

No matter what the worlds calls you, you will always and forever be my daddy. I love you. I am proud of you. I do value you, and I wouldn't trade you for the world. Even in your physical absence I have always felt your presence, guidance, and support.

Fuck em!

Destinee

ABOUT THE AUTHOR

Destinee has always understood her unique journey had a specific purpose. She has spent her life challenging the status quo and identifying a path that was uniquely hers. After spending her twenties shifting her own paradigm, Destinee has shifted her focus to sharing all that she's learned with others. In 2021, she founded the wellness platform Sle'Life centered around physical, mental, relational, and financial wellness for Women of Color. To learn more please visit www.prayslerelease.com.

CPSIA information can be obtained
at www.ICGtesting.com
Printed in the USA
BVHW020832021221
623071BV00017B/1